# In the Last Days

## A Brief Guide
## to Christ's Second Coming
## for Latter-day Saints

## Michael James Fitzgerald

overduebooks

ISBN-13: 978-1-887309-38-7

ISBN-10: 1-887309-38-1

Quantity discounts for corporations and other groups available upon request.

Michael James Fitzgerald is the author of more than 20 books which have appeared in nine languages. You can find him at michaeljamesfitzgerald.com.

# Dedication

Aubrey Claire Fitzgerald

# Table of Contents

# Preface

This brief guide is a compilation of about 30 posts I wrote from September 2014 to November 2015 for a blog called Put on the Armor of Light. It is an attempt to examine a wide variety of scriptural passages that cast light on the last days, the Second Coming of Jesus Christ, the Millennium, and the end of the world.

It is not an attempt to be authoritative or to be highly interpretive; however, it is an attempt to make sense of the events surrounding "the great and dreadful day," with an emphasis on awareness of scriptural passages rather than on fully unraveling them. I hope that you find great value in this exploration. I certainly have.

To be sure, I speak only for myself—not for the Church of Jesus Christ of Latter-day Saints or for anyone else.

## Chapter 1

# What Will Happen on the Day Christ Comes Again?

On a day not far distant, Christ Himself will return to the earth. What will that day be like?

We rely on the scriptures to tell us this story but even when we rely on the best sources, it is often difficult to see how all the pieces fit together chronologically. But there is a coherent story. I find it fascinating—riveting really.

On that incredible day there "will appear one grand sign of the Son of Man in heaven," said the Prophet Joseph Smith. "But what will the world do? They will say it is a planet, a comet, etc. But the Son of Man will come as the sign of the coming of the Son of Man, which will be as the light of morning coming out of the east" (History of the Church, 5:337; Matthew 24:27; D&C 45:36; Joseph Smith—Matthew 1:26).

On that day, we will see Him "in the clouds of heaven, clothed with power and great glory . . . with all the holy angels" (D&C 45:44). Enoch prophesied that "the Lord cometh with ten thousands of his saints, to execute judgment upon all, and to convince all that are ungodly among them of all their ungodly deeds" (Jude 1:14–15). What we will see and hear on that day will be very convincing.

When Christ comes again, it will be a day of vengeance. We read that He "shall be red in his apparel, and his garments like him that treadeth in the wine-vat" (D&C

133:48). Why will His garments be red? He answers that question for us: "I have trodden the wine-press alone, and have brought judgment upon all people; and none were with me; and I have trampled them in my fury, and I did tread upon them in mine anger, and their blood have I sprinkled upon my garments, and stained all my raiment; for this was the day of vengeance which was in my heart" (D&C 133:50–51; Isaiah 63:2–4; Revelation 19:13–15).

On that day of vengeance, "the Lord shall utter his voice, and all the ends of the earth shall hear it; and the nations of the earth shall mourn, and they that have laughed shall see their folly. And calamity shall cover the mocker, and the scorner shall be consumed; and they that have watched for iniquity shall be hewn down and cast into the fire" (D&C 45:49–50).

Unfortunately, that great day will be an unhappy day for many. "And the kings of the earth, and the great men, and the rich men, and the chief captains, and the mighty men, and every bondman, and every free man, hid themselves in the dens and in the rocks of the mountains; and [will say] to the mountains and rocks, Fall on us, and hide us from the face of him that sitteth on the throne, and from the wrath of the Lamb: for the great day of his wrath is come; and who shall be able to stand?" (Revelation 6:15–17).

Just before that time, all nations will be gathered against Jerusalem and the city will apparently be under siege. Half the city will be taken captive but "the residue of the people shall not be cut off from the city" (Zechariah 14:2).

On that glorious day, Jesus will set His foot upon the Mount of Olives, just east of Jerusalem, and there will be a great earthquake. The mountain will split in two, to the north and south, and there will be a great valley through which the residue of the Jews in Jerusalem will escape (see D&C 45:48; Zechariah 14:4–5).

On that day of great awakening, the remnant who escapes will finally recognize their King. The Lord says, "the Jews [will] look upon me and say: What are these wounds in thine hands and in thy feet? Then shall they know that I am the Lord; for I will say unto them: These wounds are the wounds with which I was wounded in the house of my friends. I am he who was lifted up. I am Jesus that was crucified. I am the Son of God. And then shall they weep because of their iniquities; then shall they lament because they persecuted their king" (D&C 45:51–53; Zechariah 13:6).

In summary, on that day of all days, Jerusalem will be under siege and half the city will be taken captive. Christ will descend with holy angels and there will be a great sign in heaven. All the ends of the earth shall hear His voice. Many shall see their own iniquity and shall attempt to hide from His wrath. He will be in red apparel for it will be a day of vengeance. His foot will touch the Mount of Olives, east of Jerusalem. There will be a great earthquake and the mountain will split in two, creating a great valley, through which the residue in Jerusalem will escape. Then they will recognize the wounds in His hands and in His feet and mourn for their iniquities and how they persecuted their true King.

I am not overconfident in my own private interpretation of these events, but as best as I can tell, this is what will happen when the arm of the Lord shall fall upon the nations on that great day (see D&C 45:47).

## Chapter 2

# The Parable of the Ten Virgins

I have no doubt that one important reason why we are "compassed about with so great a cloud of witnesses" (Hebrews 12:1) about the Second Coming of Christ is to help us prepare for it. Today is a day of preparation, a day to watch for the time when the fig tree "putteth forth [its] leaves" (see Matthew 24:32–33).

Jesus exhorted us to watch for the day of His coming because we won't know exactly when it will happen:

Watch therefore: for ye know not what hour your Lord doth come. (Matthew 24:42; compare Matthew 25:13.)

He goes on to describe a "faithful and wise servant" (see Matthew 24:45–47; compare Matthew 25:14–30) who is steadfast while his master is absent, and then an evil servant who rationalizes and says to himself, "My lord delayeth his coming."

And [he] shall begin to smite his fellowservants, and to eat and drink with the drunken; the lord of that servant shall come in a day when he looketh not for him, and in an hour that he is not aware of, and shall cut him asunder, and appoint him his portion with the hypocrites: there shall be weeping and gnashing of teeth. (Matthew 24:48–51.)

The wholly unprepared servant smites his fellowservants, eats and drinks with the drunken, and is in time appointed a portion with the hypocrites when the master returns on "a day when he looketh not for him."

We don't often associate the two, but the parables in the Matthew 25—the ten virgins, the talents, and the sheep and the goats—seem to be a continuation of the sermon in the previous chapter. Chapter 25 begins with the famous parable of the ten virgins.

Then shall the kingdom of heaven be likened unto ten virgins, which took their lamps, and went forth to meet the bridegroom. And five of them were wise, and five were foolish. They that were foolish took their lamps, and took no oil with them: but the wise took oil in their vessels with their lamps. While the bridegroom tarried, they all slumbered and slept. And at midnight there was a cry made, Behold, the bridegroom cometh; go ye out to meet him. Then all those virgins arose, and trimmed their lamps. And the foolish said unto the wise, Give us of your oil; for our lamps are gone out. But the wise answered, saying, Not so; lest there be not enough for us and you: but go ye rather to them that sell, and buy for yourselves. And while they went to buy, the bridegroom came; and they that were ready went in with him to the marriage: and the door was shut. Afterward came also the other virgins, saying, Lord, Lord, open to us. But he answered and said, Verily I say unto you, I know you not. Watch therefore, for ye know neither the day nor the hour wherein the Son of man cometh. (Matthew 25:1–13.)

When I was a new convert, I used to wonder why the wise virgins couldn't give the unwise oil for their lamps? As I grew older I discovered that it was because there are certain things we absolutely cannot do for others and that others cannot do for us. Others may pray for us, but they can't do our praying for us. Others may try to teach us, but they can't study the scriptures for us. Each of us must become a disciple on our own terms. In order for our discipleship to be meaningful and lasting, we have to do those things for ourselves, for the right reasons.

# Chapter 3

# September 2015

September 2015 was an interesting month. Several astronomical events fell on the same days as holy days on the Hebrew calendar. I'll let you decide if these events are significant in regard to the Last Days or not. Let's take a tour of the month and see what happened.

Rosh Hashanah (השנה ראש), or Jewish New Year, is also known as the Feast of the Trumpets. It began at sundown on Sunday, September 13, 2015. This holiday occurs on the first two days of the month Tishrei, which is the seventh month of the Jewish calendar. Lenet Hadley Reed wrote an article entitled "The Golden Plates and the Feast of the Trumpets" in the January 2000 *Ensign*. I recommend it.

The days between Rosh Hashanah and Yom Kippur are called the Days of Awe. A partial solar eclipse occurred on September 13, 2015, though it was only visible in certain areas of the southern hemisphere.

The shemitah is the seventh or sabbatical year, a year of rest for the land according to Exodus 23:10–11:

> And six years thou shalt sow thy land, and shalt gather in the fruits thereof: but the seventh year thou shalt let it rest and lie still; that the poor of thy people may eat: and what they leave the beasts of the field shall eat. In like manner thou shalt deal with thy vineyard, and with thy oliveyard.

Some controversy exists about when the next sabbatical year will fall, but according to the *Encyclopaedia Judaica, Second Edition* ([Thomson Gale, 2006], 623–628), the shemitah began in 2014 and will end this year. (See Leviticus 25:1–7, 18–22; Deuteronomy 15:1–6; also see the entry on the sabbatical year in the Bible Dictionary.)

After seven times seven years comes the fiftieth or jubilee year (see Leviticus 25:8–17; see also the Bible Dictionary entry on the jubilee year). Some believe that 2015/2016 will be the 70th jubilee year since the nation of Israel entered the land of Canaan. However, there is much dissension about calendar dates so I will not go out on a limb here.

Yom Kippur (הכיפורים יום) or the Day of Atonement began at sundown on Tuesday, September 22, 2015. For Jews, this holiday is the holiest day of the year, a day of fasting, prayer, and repentance.

Joseph Smith, by the way, received the plates of gold from the angel Moroni 188 years ago on this day; however, September 22, 1827, fell on the same day as the Rosh Hashanah or the Feast of Trumpets that year.

Sukkot (סֻכּוֹת) or the Feast of the Tabernacles or Booths began at sundown on Sunday, September 27, 2015. A total lunar eclipse occurred during the evening of September 27, 2015. If you live in northern Utah, for example, the eclipse will reach its apex at 8:47 p.m. Mountain Daylight Time.

By the way, September 27, 2015 is important to me personally: I heard the first missionary discussion 40 years ago on this day—and it stuck!

The dates of the holy days and the eclipses are astronomical certainties. The Lord gave the "lights in the firmament . . . for signs, and for seasons, and for days, and years" (see Genesis 1:14) so there may be significance to these phenomena. But the dates for the shemitah and jubilee are not so certain.

When someone makes bold claims as to the exact date of a prophesied event, well, I am careful not to board a train for which God has not given me a ticket. But it's always good to be aware and watching. As the Savior warned, "Watch therefore: for ye know not what hour your Lord doth come" (Matthew 24:42).

# Chapter 4

# Upon My House Shall It Begin

In the last days, our days, darkness will prevail on the earth and all flesh will become corrupt, in spite of technological advances and an explosion of information. Just when knowledge and information flourish, so does self-deception and unbelief through the universal sin of pride. Doesn't this contrast seem strange? It's like we're starving to death while standing in the middle of a fully stocked grocery store.

To me, the best way to explain this contradiction was given by Jesus Himself when, one night in or near Jerusalem, He had a conversation with a Jewish leader named Nicodemus:

> And this is the condemnation, that light is come into the world, and men loved darkness rather than light, *because their deeds were evil.* For every one that doeth evil hateth the light, neither cometh to the light, lest his deeds should be reproved. (John 3:19, 20; emphasis added.)

Jesus lays out the issue straightforwardly: men prefer darkness over light and they don't want to come to the light for fear that they'll be found out. Hence, darkness prevails.

According to the scriptures, it's going to get worse before it gets better, though individual results may vary.

This darkness will be put to flight by the remarkable appearance of our Lord Jesus Christ when, like a whirlwind, vengeance, wrath, and desolation will descend upon all the face of the earth.

Verily, verily, I say unto you, darkness covereth the earth, and gross darkness the minds of the people [see Isaiah 60:2], and all flesh has become corrupt before my face. Behold, vengeance cometh speedily upon the inhabitants of the earth, a day of wrath, a day of burning, a day of desolation, of weeping, of mourning, and of lamentation; and as a whirlwind it shall come upon all the face of the earth, saith the Lord. And upon my house shall it begin, and from my house shall it go forth, saith the Lord; first among those among you, saith the Lord, who have professed to know my name and have not known me, and have blasphemed against me in the midst of my house, saith the Lord. (D&C 112:23–26; emphasis added.)

The interesting point is, this wrath and desolation will begin at the house of God, meaning, I believe, the household of God or His Church. Peter strengthens this assertion by offering this prophesy in his first epistle:

For the time is come that judgment must begin at the house of God: and if it first begin at us, what shall the end be of them that obey not the gospel of God? (1 Peter 4:17; emphasis added.)

Sadly, it appears that the long-prophesied judgment and destruction will "first begin at us," most likely among the hypocrites "in the midst of [His] house" (D&C 112:26). And who can claim to not be a hypocrite? Aren't we all, at least to some degree? Gulp.

Takeaways? I don't really know what all this means or how it will happen, but I believe from the context that something will happen before or perhaps at Christ's coming to those in His church who are not living the gospel as they should live it, who may perhaps be socially attached but without being spiritually attached to their faith, who are covering their sins, lest they be reproved (see John 3:20).

We've got some work to do. I certainly do.

To me, several signs that herald this are (1) when members of Christ's church persist in serious and secret transgression and don't rely on the Atonement of Christ daily, (2) when they persecute other members of His Church for living the gospel more circumspectly than they do themselves—internal persecution—and (3) when members of the Church rise up against the prophets because of what I call "social righteousness."

That's my view. It's a limited view to be sure. But I see these things happening before my eyes. I'm sure you do too. We're going to see more and more of this. On the other hand, we'll also see faithful saints endure these trials and become closer to the Lord because of them.

# Chapter 5

# The Disintegration of the Family

Twenty years ago, the First Presidency and the Council of the Twelve Apostles published "The Family: A Proclamation to the World." President Hinckley shared it for the first time at a general Relief Society meeting on September 23, 1995. He gave it as part of a talk entitled, "Stand Strong against the Wiles of the Devil." Before he read the proclamation publicly, he introduced it with these words:

> With so much of sophistry that is passed off as truth, with so much of deception concerning standards and values, with so much of allurement and enticement to take on the slow stain of the world, we have felt to warn and forewarn. In furtherance of this we of the First Presidency and the Council of the Twelve Apostles now issue a proclamation to the Church and to the world as a declaration and reaffirmation of standards, doctrines, and practices relative to the family which the prophets, seers, and revelators of this church have repeatedly stated throughout its history.

To me the most chilling sentence in the document is near the end: "Further, we warn that the disintegration of the family will bring upon individuals, communities, and nations the calamities foretold by ancient and modern prophets."

How has the traditional family held up in recent years? Here are a few telling indicators. I'll let you judge and draw your own conclusions about these statistics.

- In 2013, more than 41 percent of births in the United States were to unmarried women. The number was 5 percent in 1960. The following analyses of this trend comes from the Child Trends data bank and cites 15 studies:

  > Children born to unmarried mothers are more likely to grow up in a single-parent household, experience instable living arrangements, live in poverty, and have socio-emotional problems. . . . As these children reach adolescence, they are more likely to have low educational attainment, engage in sex at a younger age, and have a birth outside of marriage. . . . As young adults, children born outside of marriage are more likely to be idle (neither in school nor employed), have lower occupational status and income, and have more troubled marriages and more divorces than those born to married parents. . . .

- Between 1973 and 2011, some 53 million legal abortions took place in the United States. In 2011, 85.5 percent of abortions were performed for unmarried women.
- In spite of some statistics to the contrary, divorce rates have not declined but continue to be high though these rates may have flattened because younger people tend to wait longer to get married and cohabitation is now commonplace.

- Last fall (2014), the marriage rate reached a 93-year low with a rate of 50.3 percent for Americans ages 18 and older (this rate includes same-sex couples). The highest marriage rate occurred in 1960 when it reached 72.2 percent.
- A synopsis of the book The Growth of Incarceration in the United States: Exploring Causes and Consequences (The National Academies Press, 2014) states:

> The rate of imprisonment in the United States more than quadrupled during the last four decades. The U.S. penal population of 2.2 million adults is by far the largest in the world. Just under one-quarter of the world's prisoners are held in American prisons. The U.S. rate of incarceration, with nearly 1 out of every 100 adults in prison or jail, is 5 to 10 times higher than the rates in Western Europe and other democracies. The U.S. prison population is largely drawn from the most disadvantaged part of the nation's population: mostly men under age 40, disproportionately minority, and poorly educated. Prisoners often carry additional deficits of drug and alcohol addictions, mental and physical illnesses, and lack of work preparation or experience.

- Between 2007 and 2014, a Pew Research report shows that those claiming to be unaffiliated with any religion grew from 16.1 to 22.8 percent, an increase of 6.7 percent, while Catholics and evangelical and mainline Protestants declined in numbers.

In His Sermon on the Mount, Christ asked, "Do men gather grapes of thorns, or figs of thistles?" (see Matthew 7:16). In other words, "Can you pluck sweet fruit from noxious weeds?" The answer is, of course, no. Weeds prosper when the garden is neglected, and many families in the early 21st century are withering.

Stable families are the foundation of a stable society. Without strong, united families, society will unravel. I believe that, though much of society may unravel, many traditional families from all walks of life will remain intact and strong until the Savior appears, and that those families will be a means of spiritual and physical survival for many who are standing on the earth on that great and dreadful day.

# Chapter 6

# The Constitution on the Brink of Ruin

The Prophet Joseph Smith prophesied that the day would come when the Constitution of the United States would be in great jeopardy. (I am not speaking of the White Horse Prophecy but of other, historically reliable statements made by the Prophet and others.) I see this event as one of the signs of the Second Coming.

I believe that the Constitution of our land is a living document and that it may be adapted and has been adapted according to the voice of the people. There are provisions in the Constitution itself for making such changes. Those kinds of changes—the kind that follow due process—don't trouble me.

How and in what way the Constitution of the United States will be pushed to the brink, I won't venture to guess; however, I have watched with interest the administrative and judicial challenges to the Constitution that have arisen in recent years. No doubt we will yet see many tests of the elasticity of this incredibly important document.

Who is the real source of the Constitution? The Lord states in the Doctrine and Covenants that the Constitution was established by Him and "by the hands of wise men whom [He] raised up [for] this very purpose":

> The laws and constitution of the people . . . I have suffered to be established, and should be

maintained for the rights and protection of all flesh, according to just and holy principles; that every man may act in doctrine and principle pertaining to futurity, according to the moral agency which I have given unto him, that every man may be accountable for his own sins in the day of judgment. . . . And for this purpose have I established the Constitution of this land, by the hands of wise men whom I raised up unto this very purpose, and redeemed the land by the shedding of blood. (D&C 101:77,78,80.)

I have no doubt that the Constitution made it possible for the gospel to be restored some 40 years after it was accepted by this nation as the supreme law of the land.

But how or when will the Constitution falter? We have in the handwriting of Martha Jane Knowlton Coray and Larinda Pratt Weihe the following statement uttered by the Prophet Joseph on July 19, 1840, when he was just 34 years old (that's 175 years ago today):

Even this nation [the United States] will be on the very verge of crumbling to pieces and tumbling to the ground and when the Constitution is upon the brink of ruin this people will be the Staff up[on] which the Nation shall lean and they shall bear the Constitution away from the very verge of destruction. . . . (See also "I Have a Question," Ensign, June 1976.)

Eliza R. Snow said of this statement or of a similar statement:

I heard the prophet say, 'The time will come when the government of these United States will be so nearly overthrown through its corruption, that the Constitution will hang as it were by a single hair, and the Latter-day Saints—the Elders of Israel—will step forward to its rescue and save it.' (From Journal History, MSF 143 #28, July 24, 1871; see also "I Have a Question," Ensign, June 1976.)

I was sitting in the Marriott Center on the BYU campus on September 16, 1986 and heard these words from the mouth of Ezra Taft Benson with my own ears:

> I have faith that the Constitution will be saved as prophesied by Joseph Smith. But it will not be saved in Washington. It will be saved by the citizens of this nation who love and cherish freedom. It will be saved by enlightened members of this Church—men and women who will subscribe to and abide by the principles of the Constitution.

It's not my purpose to speculate how this will or could happen. My only hope is that by sharing sturdy and verifiable quotes and facts regarding the last times, readers will feel forearmed and better prepared for the second appearing of Jesus Christ.

But let me say this much: I feel strongly that the Constitution will suffer when the majority of voices in this nation cry out for iniquity. Let me close with these words of Mosiah, warning his people of a day to come:

> If the time comes that the voice of the people doth choose iniquity, then is the time that the judgments of God will come upon you; yea, then is the time he will visit you with great destruction even as he has hitherto visited this land. (Mosiah 29:27.)

# Chapter 7

# Natural Disasters

A few days ago, I saw this headline from CBS News and sort of chuckled: "Big earthquakes double in 2014, but scientists say they're not linked." Here's a quote for the article: "We have recently experienced a period that has had one of the highest rates of great earthquakes ever recorded," said lead study author Tom Parsons, a research geophysicist with the U.S. Geological Survey (USGS) in Menlo Park, California. But even though the global earthquake rate is on the rise, the number of quakes can still be explained by random chance, said Parsons and co-author Eric Geist, also a USGS researcher (emphasis mine).

Yes, from a scientific standpoint, these earthquakes may appear random, but from a prophetic point of view, they come as no surprise: scripture tells us that there will be "earthquakes in divers places" leading up to the time of Christ's second advent (Mark 13:8; see also Matthew 24:7; Luke 21:11; Mormon 8:30; D&C 45:33; Joseph Smith—Matthew 1:29.)

In fact, according to John's revelation, there will be a great earthquake at the time of Christ's Second Coming:

> And there were voices, and thunders, and lightnings; and there was a great earthquake, such as was not since men were upon the earth, so mighty an earthquake, and so great. And the great city was divided into three parts, and the cities of the nations fell: and great Babylon came in remembrance before God, to give unto her the

cup of the wine of the fierceness of his wrath. And every island fled away, and the mountains were not found. (Revelation 16:18–20; compare Zechariah 14:4–5; emphasis added.)

Other calamities will mark the time. Here is as complete a list as I can find:

- Thunderings
- Lightnings
- Tempests (hurricanes, cyclones, tornadoes, and so forth)
- Famines
- Great hailstorms (add to that snowstorms, such as the one in Buffalo in late 2014)
- Famines (including droughts)
- Pestilences (epidemic diseases—Ebola comes to mind)
- Waves of the sea heaving beyond their bounds (tsunamis, for example)

Modern scripture, for example, tells of a great hailstorm in the last days:

And there shall be a great hailstorm sent forth to destroy the crops of the earth. (D&C 29:16.)

And ancient scripture supports it:

And there fell upon men a great hail out of heaven, every stone about the weight of a talent: and men blasphemed God because of the plague of the hail; for the plague thereof was exceeding great. (Revelation 16:21.)

All these disasters will be a testimony to those on earth to get ready for the great and dreadful day:

> And after your testimony cometh wrath and indignation upon the people. For after your testimony cometh the testimony of earthquakes, that shall cause groanings in the midst of her, and men shall fall upon the ground and shall not be able to stand. And also cometh the testimony of the voice of thunderings, and the voice of lightnings, and the voice of tempests, and the voice of the waves of the sea heaving themselves beyond their bounds. And all things shall be in commotion; and surely, men's hearts shall fail them; for fear shall come upon all people. (D&C 88:88–91; see also D&C 43:25.

I believe that natural disasters will increase in number and severity from now until "when the Son of man shall come in his glory, and all the holy angels with him" (Matthew 25:31).

We would be wise to watch for the day. I'm not saying that day is tomorrow, but I believe it will come sooner than some would like.

# Chapter 8

# Food Storage

A few years ago, I was with my family at an outdoor event in Salt Lake City. I think we had just passed some sort of preparedness booth when one of us overheard someone say, "I'm not worried about an earthquake. If anything happens, the Mormons will take care of us."

I'm sure Latter-day Saints will do their best to help their neighbors, but I also think it best to do all we can to prepare ourselves.

Latter-day Saints have been counseled for years to store food. I believe this prophetic counsel is inspired and we have, since we were first married, stored food for our proverbial rainy day.

I am not going to explore the how of food storage in this chapter, or even the why, but rather what are some possible reasons you might really be happy you had stored food for your family.

I am not trying to scare anyone. I am just offering a reality check. Here goes. I promise it's not uplifting.

- Income disruption
- Job loss
- Disability
- Death of breadwinner
- Transportation and travel issues or restrictions
- Food contamination
- Famine, drought, blight, or infestation

- Economic panic, loss, or collapse
- Quarantine due to epidemic disease and pestilence
- Political unrest
- Religious persecution
- Rampant crime
- Anarchy
- Electromagnetic pulse attack
- War
- Martial law
- Natural disaster—earthquakes, floods, storms, solar flares, and so forth

You could probably add an item or two to the list. We could see one or more of these events happen before our eyes, in rapid succession.

What would you do? What will you do to prepare today? The next thing we plan to do is to take an inventory of what food we have and make a list of things we want to add. Soon.

# Chapter 9

# A Desolating Sickness

Before the Second Coming of Christ, an overflowing or desolating scourge—a desolating sickness—will be poured out from time to time upon the earth. Shortly before the Babylonian captivity of Jerusalem, Isaiah prophesied to scornful men who ruled the once holy city (see Isaiah 28:14):

> Because ye have said, We have made a covenant with death, and with hell are we at agreement; when the overflowing scourge shall pass through, it shall not come unto us . . . [but] your covenant with death shall be disannulled, and your agreement with hell shall not stand; when the overflowing scourge shall pass through, then ye shall be trodden down by it. (Isaiah 28:15, 18.)

When mortals boast that they can escape death of themselves, God is obliged to disabuse them of the notion. On several occasions, such as in 588 B.C. and 70 A.D, He has flattened Jerusalem when the people of that city rejected and killed the prophets including, ultimately, the Son of God.

A scourge, according to Merriam-Webster, is "a cause of wide or great affliction," but it appears from latter-day scripture that this scourge is more than an affliction: it will lead to the death of many souls "until the earth is empty":

> For a desolating scourge shall go forth among the inhabitants of the earth, and shall continue to be poured out from time to time, if they repent not,

until the earth is empty, and the inhabitants
thereof are consumed away and utterly destroyed
by the brightness of my coming. (D&C 5:19.)

Later in modern scripture we read:

And there shall be men standing in that
generation, that shall not pass until they shall see
an overflowing scourge; for a desolating sickness
shall cover the land. (D&C 45:31.)

Here the Lord tells us that the scourge will be a
desolating sickness that will cover the land. It is easy to
imagine, given recent news, that a disease or series of
diseases could get out of control and take thousands
even millions of lives, in spite of the frantic efforts of
modern medicine.

The knowledge and wisdom of men cannot save us
from the decrees of God which will remain in force
unless the inhabitants of the earth repent. Given what we
know, that repentance is not likely. But one can hope.

# Chapter 10

# Secret Combinations

The phrases secret combination or secret combinations appear 20 times in the standard works, mostly in the Book of Mormon. A secret combination is a pact between two or more parties to commit criminal acts, usually violent, under a cloak of secrecy—often involving secret societies and the exchange of oaths and signs—for gain, power, and the glory of this world.

Probably the first secret combination was made between Satan and Cain who slew his brother Abel in order to obtain his flocks. The annihilation of the Jaredite and Nephite peoples who once lived on the American continents were precipitated and accelerated by secret combinations, as Moroni explains:

> And it came to pass that they formed a secret combination, even as they of old; which combination is most abominable and wicked above all, in the sight of God; for the Lord worketh not in secret combinations, neither doth he will that man should shed blood, but in all things hath forbidden it, from the beginning of man. And now I, Moroni, do not write the manner of their oaths and combinations, for it hath been made known unto me that they are had among all people, and they are had among the Lamanites. And they have caused the destruction of this people of whom I am now speaking, and also the destruction of the people of Nephi. And whatsoever nation shall uphold such secret combinations, to get power and gain, until they

shall spread over the nation, behold, they shall be destroyed; for the Lord will not suffer that the blood of his saints, which shall be shed by them, shall always cry unto him from the ground for vengeance upon them and yet he avenge them not. (Ether 8:18–22; emphasis added)

In 1833, the Lord explained that He gave the Word of Wisdom "in consequence of evils and designs which do and will exist in the hearts of conspiring men in the last days" (D&C 89:4). This also suggests the possible presence of secret combinations. Let me explain.

In the revelation known as section 89 of the Doctrine and Covenants, the Lord counsels us against using such addictive substances as alcohol and tobacco. It seems that the modern businesses that purvey these and other addictive and harmful substances have likely been cooked up by "conspiring men" for gain, under the protection of local and national laws. I am assured that such businesses will cease to exist when Christ reigns supreme over this earth again.

I am not much on conspiracy theories and I don't wish to delve into or postulate on them, but I constantly see evidence of coalitions of evil intent which the scriptures describe as secret combinations. I fear they will become so widespread that they will prove the near overthrow or near entire destruction of families, corporations, governments, societies, even civilization itself, before the Lord comes again. But they will not succeed.

# Chapter 11

# Men's Hearts Shall Fail Them

We live in a violent world. I think it's always been a dangerous place, at least since Cain's rebellion. But it's getting worse. Much worse.

I don't read much news—it's sickening to me—but I am exposed to it nonetheless, usually through social media. I'm not burying my head in the sand. I'm hiding my heart from the iniquity that abounds in this fallen and falling world (see Matthew 24:12). I can hardly stand it.

Every day, I am crushed by news reports of shootings and other vulgar, senseless crimes. The most troubling are those committed against children. Then there are disasters, wars, and the endless human suffering that follows.

Who can take it all in? I wonder how much longer God can stand it, much less us.

It isn't like we haven't been warned. Jesus foretold of a perplexing time when men's hearts would fail them for fear:

> And there shall be signs in the sun, and in the moon, and in the stars; and upon the earth distress of nations, with perplexity; the sea and the waves roaring; men's hearts failing them for fear, and for looking after those things which are coming on the earth: for the powers of heaven shall be shaken. (Luke 21:25–26; emphasis added.)

I don't think He was talking about a medical condition requiring bypass surgery. He's talking about an emotional or spiritual failure caused by sin, crime, and other frightful world events.

> And all things shall be in commotion; and surely, men's hearts shall fail them; for fear shall come upon all people. (D&C 88:91; see also D&C 45:26 and Moses 7:66; emphasis added.)

Like a great monster, fear could consume us, swallow us whole. But there is a remedy, a way out. The admonition to "fear not" appears over and over in the scriptures. It's an admonition to have faith, trust God, and be patient, especially in times of trouble as in our day.

> For I the Lord thy God will hold thy right hand, saying unto thee, Fear not; I will help thee. (Isaiah 41:13.)

> Fear not: for they that be with us are more than they that be with them. (2 Kings 6:16.)

> Verily I say unto you my friends, fear not, let your hearts be comforted; yea, rejoice evermore, and in everything give thanks. (D&C 98:1.)

Moroni warned us that "despair cometh because of iniquity" (see Moroni 10:22), but in the next breath he promised:

> And Christ truly said unto our fathers: If ye have faith ye can do all things which are expedient unto me. (Moroni 10:23.)

A modern apostle, Howard W. Hunter, offered these comforting words:

> If our lives and our faith are centered upon Jesus Christ and his restored gospel, nothing can ever go

permanently wrong. On the other hand, if our lives are not centered on the Savior and his teachings, no other success can ever be permanently right.

We live in a time of iniquity and despair, but it is also a time of great hope. It's possible to move forward every day with "a perfect brightness of hope" (see 2 Nephi 31:20) though it requires a firm mind and constant positive action. In other words, real faith. The real deal.

This chilling reminder from the First Presidency and the Quorum of the Twelve comes to mind: "We warn that the disintegration of the family will bring upon individuals, communities, and nations the calamities foretold by ancient and modern prophets."

Our hope need not disintegrate though families and the world itself disintegrate around us. Yes, violence and persecution rage, but we can endure it.

And ye shall be hated of all men for my name's sake: but he that endureth to the end shall be saved. (Matthew 10:22.)

It won't be long. We know for certain that it won't be too long.

And except those days should be shortened, there should no flesh be saved: but for the elect's sake those days shall be shortened. (Matthew 24:22.)

Hang on. Hold on. Hope on. It will all work out. Embrace your faith as you would your child in a tornado. Above all else, keep looking up.

I will lift up mine eyes unto the hills, from whence cometh my help. (Psalms 121:1.)

# Chapter 12

# Eating and Drinking, Marrying and Giving in Marriage

In previous chapters, I've talked a lot about the difficult conditions and frightening events that will lead up to Christ's advent. But here in contrast is an interesting passage to consider:

> But as the days of Noe were, so shall also the coming of the Son of man be. For as in the days that were before the flood they were eating and drinking, marrying and giving in marriage, until the day that Noe entered into the ark, and knew not until the flood came, and took them all away; so shall also the coming of the Son of man be. (Matthew 24:37–39; emphasis added.)

That is, in spite of upheaval in the last days, life will continue on as it always has to a degree. We'll eat, drink, marry, have children, and pay the mortgage and on and on. In some ways, life will seem as it always has, although many events that we witness, either near or far, will be petrifying. Perhaps this is why the Second Coming will overtake us as "a thief in the night." We'll be preoccupied and won't see it coming.

In His Olivet discourse, the Savior spoke of the evil servant who will be caught off guard:

> But and if that evil servant shall say in his heart, My lord delayeth his coming; and shall begin to smite his fellowservants, and to eat and drink with the drunken; the lord of that servant shall come in

a day when he looketh not for him, and in an hour that he is not aware of, and shall cut him asunder, and appoint him his portion with the hypocrites: there shall be weeping and gnashing of teeth. (Matthew 24:48–51; emphasis added.)

Though devastation may be widespread, the entire earth will not be a smoldering heap when Christ comes. There may be a hint of normalcy around us, and the spiritually drowsy will not perceive the signs readily if at all.

I don't know what normal will look like in those days but it will be normal enough to catch many off guard.

Watch ye therefore: for ye know not when the master of the house cometh, at even, or at midnight, or at the cockcrowing, or in the morning: lest coming suddenly he find you sleeping. And what I say unto you I say unto all, Watch. (Mark 13:35–37.)

# Chapter 13

# The Mark of the Beast

The Book of Revelation, in chapter 13, talks of "the mark, or the name of the beast" which is "the number of a man." I'm sure you've heard of the mystical number 666. Speculation on what the mark and the number 666 mean is endless.

I'm not a big fan of speculation. It feels empty to me. It's overly complex and often shoots beyond the mark, way beyond. But we can follow a higher road by taking the Holy Spirit as our guide (see D&C 45:57), not the wild, overly self-assured, endless speculations of men.

I am only going to cite a few verses that discuss the mark and comment on what those scriptures say. The important thing to me is that we become aware of what the scriptures say about the Second Coming, not what they fully mean. We will know that in time. Everyone will, whether they like it or not.

The headnote of chapter 13 reads:

> John sees fierce-looking beasts that represent
> degenerate earthly kingdoms controlled by
> Satan—The devil works miracles and deceives
> men. (Emphasis added.)

Satan's influence will dominate nations, and corrupt rulers of nations, in the last days. This beast mentioned in the passage that follows (and there are lots of beasts in Revelation) appears to be a political leader who makes everyone receive a mark on their foreheads or on their right hand:

And he causeth all, both small and great, rich and poor, free and bond, to receive a mark in their right hand, or in their foreheads: and that no man might buy or sell, save he that had the mark, or the name of the beast, or the number of his name. Here is wisdom. Let him that hath understanding count the number of the beast: for it is the number of a man; and his number is Six hundred threescore and six [666]. (Revelation 13:16–18; emphasis added.)

Here's the basic idea: If you don't have this mark, you won't be able to buy or sell—or, rather, to participate in commerce. If you cannot participate in commerce, it will be rather difficult to make a living or to live a normal life. So the inducement to take this mark upon you will be strong, as is the inducement to prepare now.

But the mark also seems to symbolize an allegiance to idolatry or to the worship of a false god or idol and at the last day, such allegiance will come with a price:

And the third angel followed them, saying with a loud voice, If any man worship the beast and his image, and receive his mark in his forehead, or in his hand, the same shall drink of the wine of the wrath of God, which is poured out without mixture into the cup of his indignation; and he shall be tormented with fire and brimstone in the presence of the holy angels, and in the presence of the Lamb: and the smoke of their torment ascendeth up for ever and ever: and they have no rest day nor night, who worship the beast and his image, and whosoever receiveth the mark of his name. (Revelation 14:9–11; see also Revelation 16:2; 19:19–21; emphasis added.)

For those who overcome the beast and his mark, there is a far better destiny, even a place in the celestial world:

> And I saw as it were a sea of glass mingled with fire: and them that had gotten the victory over the beast, and over his image, and over his mark, and over the number of his name, stand on the sea of glass, having the harps of God. (Revelation 15:2; see also Revelation 20:4; emphasis added.)

I am not going to offer an interpretation of these verses, only some advice: Watch to see if political leaders, governments, and nations tighten their grip on commerce in such a way that it forces people to compromise their faith and allegiance to God. I don't even allow myself to guess at this point what countries or who may be involved. I am not implying who and where and when. I am only advising to watch, be wary, and prepare.

I find comfort in these words from the Doctrine and Covenants about standing "independent above all other creatures":

> That through my providence, notwithstanding the tribulation which shall descend upon you, that the church may stand independent above all other creatures beneath the celestial world; that you may come up unto the crown prepared for you, and be made rulers over many kingdoms, saith the Lord God, the Holy One of Zion. . . . (D&C 78:14–15.)

Now is a great time to prepare.

**Note**: For an interesting and reliable discussion of the symbols in Revelation, see Richard D. Draper's

"Understanding Images and Symbols in the Book of Revelation." See footnote 41.

# Chapter 14

# The Antichrist

Shortly before His death, Jesus told His apostles that false Christs and false prophets would deceive even His chosen followers:

> There shall arise false Christs, and false prophets, and shall shew great signs and wonders; insomuch that, if it were possible, they shall deceive the very elect. (Matthew 24:24; see also Mark 13:22.)

The apostle John wrote in his first epistle about antichrists:

> Little children, it is the last time: and as ye have heard that antichrist shall come, even now are there many antichrists; whereby we know that it is the last time. ... Who is a liar but he that denieth that Jesus is the Christ? He is antichrist, that denieth the Father and the Son. (1 John 2:18,22; compare 2 John 1:7.)

Here John tells us that an "antichrist shall come" but also that there are many antichrists. According to the Bible Dictionary, an antichrist is "one who would assume the guise of Christ but in reality would be opposed to Christ . . . [or] anyone or anything that counterfeits the true gospel or plan of salvation and that openly or secretly is set up in opposition to Christ."

It's hard to imagine a worse kind of dishonesty. I mean, what kind of people dream these kinds of schemes up? Maybe that's why there's an outer darkness. No one can deal with such folks so you have to send them off to deal with themselves. The ultimate time out.

Several notable antichrists are in the Book of Mormon such as Sherem, Nehor, and Korihor.

John also wrote:

> And every spirit that confesseth not that Jesus Christ is come in the flesh is not of God: and this is that spirit of antichrist, whereof ye have heard that it should come; and even now already is it in the world. (1 John 4:3.)

So, if someone won't confess that Jesus Christ is come in the flesh, is that the spirit of antichrist? Yes, I think it is.

While there may be many antichrists, it also appears that there will be one in particular who will get a lot of attention. Though Satan is the great antichrist, he will also promote a prominent mortal imposter.

Paul wrote to the Thessalonians of a "man of sin" who will appear sometime before the Second Coming of the Son of Man. This character is considered by many as the Antichrist.

> Let no man deceive you by any means: for that day shall not come, except there come a falling away first, and that man of sin be revealed, the son of perdition; who opposeth and exalteth himself above all that is called God, or that is worshipped; so that he as God sitteth in the temple of God, shewing himself that he is God. And then shall that Wicked be revealed, whom the Lord shall consume with the spirit of his mouth, and shall destroy with the brightness of his coming: even

him, whose coming is after the working of Satan
with all power and signs and lying wonders, and
with all deceivableness of unrighteousness in them
that perish; because they received not the love of
the truth, that they might be saved. (2
Thessalonians 2:3–4,8–10.)

In the Book of Revelation, John writes of a beast who:

Doeth great wonders, so that he maketh fire come
down from heaven on the earth in the sight of
men, and deceiveth them that dwell on the earth
by the means of those miracles which he had
power to do in the sight of the beast; saying to
them that dwell on the earth, that they should
make an image to the beast, which had the wound
by a sword, and did live. And he had power to give
life unto the image of the beast, that the image of
the beast should both speak, and cause that as
many as would not worship the image of the beast
should be killed. (Revelation 13:11–15).

I won't attempt here to untangle the details around this
beast, or the "first beast" (v. 12), or the "false prophet"
who is in partnership with the beast to deceive the world
(see Revelation 16:13 and 20:10). But I will mention that
the beast here spoken of is also the beast who will
impose a mark of commerce ("the mark of the beast")
that I have written about earlier.

Suffice it to say that in the last days:

- There will be many who will deny Christ and the
  Father.
- There will also be those who pretend to be
  Christ or prophets.

- Among the imposters will be those who show great and deceptive signs.
- One particular double-dealer, the man of sin or, popularly, the Antichrist, will be prominent and troublesome.
- He will be in cahoots with others to deceive the world and bring them into subservience, even killing those who do not worship the image of the beast.
- This antichrist, and those who support his craft, will be consumed at Christ's coming.

I am not asking you—not here or in any of my writings on the Second Coming—to take my word on the subject. I do encourage you, however, to be well-informed, to study the scriptures linked here, among others, and to draw your own conclusions. I don't ever try to over-interpret the events leading up to Christ's second advent, but I do want to know about them and understand them as best I can so that I will be ready to face them. That's my hope for you too.

# Chapter 15

# The Abomination of Desolation

A few days before His death and resurrection, Jesus gave this warning in what is known as the Olivet discourse:

> When ye therefore shall see the abomination of desolation, spoken of by Daniel the prophet, stand in the holy place, (whoso readeth, let him understand:) then let them which be in Judæa flee into the mountains. (Matthew 24:15–16; emphasis added; compare Mark 13:14 and Luke 21:20–21.)

What is this "abomination of desolation"? I will do my best to explain.

Daniel the prophet, who lived six or seven centuries before Christ, foretold this event or phenomena, as Christ indicated in His prophecy:

> And arms shall stand on his part, and they shall pollute the sanctuary of strength, and shall take away the daily sacrifice, and they shall place the abomination that maketh desolate. (Daniel 11:31; emphasis added; compare Daniel 9:27; 12:11.)

The abomination that "they shall place" was a pagan idol set up in the temple of Jerusalem, according to the apocryphal book of 1 Maccabees. This book records the invasion of the city by the marauding forces of the Greek king Antiochus Epiphanes in the autumn of 162 BC (approximate):

> Now the fifteenth day of the month Casleu [Kislev in the Hebrew calendar], in the hundred forty and fifth year, they set up the abomination of desolation upon the

altar, and builded idol altars throughout the cities of Juda on every side; and burnt incense at the doors of their houses, and in the streets. (1 Maccabees 1:54-55.)

This prophecy and its fulfillment also speak of a time when Jerusalem will be compassed and besieged by invading armies, as by the Roman emperor Titus who destroyed city and the temple in 70 AD and in the last days, just before the coming of Christ (compare Joseph Smith—Matthew 1:12 and Joseph Smith—Matthew 1:32).

Jeremiah also spoke of the desolation that will occur because of Israel's abominations, just prior to the Babylonian captivity and destruction of Jerusalem and Solomon's temple in approximately 587–588 BC:

The Lord could no longer bear, because of the evil of your doings, and because of the abominations which ye have committed; therefore is your land a desolation, and an astonishment, and a curse, without an inhabitant, as at this day. (Jeremiah 44:22; emphasis added.)

Ezekiel, a contemporary of Jeremiah, spoke similarly:

Then shall they know that I am the Lord, when I have laid the land most desolate because of all their abominations which they have committed. (Ezekiel 33:29; emphasis added.)

Modern revelation speaks of the desolation of abomination or wrath of God which will fall upon wicked:

Therefore, tarry ye, and labor diligently, that you may be perfected in your ministry to go forth among the Gentiles for the last time, as many as the mouth of the Lord shall name, to bind up the law and seal up the testimony, and to prepare the saints for the hour of judgment which is to come; that their souls may escape the wrath of God, the desolation of abomination which awaits the wicked, both in this world and in the world to come. Verily, I say unto you, let those who are not the first elders continue in the vineyard until the mouth of the Lord shall call them, for their time is not yet come; their garments are not clean from the blood of this generation. (D&C 88:84–85; emphasis added; see also D&C 84:117.)

Therefore, the abomination of desolation speaks of at least these three things: (1) the desecration of the holy temple by setting up of an idol in its precincts, (2) Jerusalem being besieged by foreign or invading armies, and (3) a punishment of the wicked.

It has happened before and it will take place again during a siege of Jerusalem that will occur just before Christ at His Second Coming will set His foot upon the Mount of Olives.

## Chapter 16

# Flee unto Zion for Safety

To me, one of the most fascinating—and comforting—prophecies about the time previous to the Second Coming of our Savior tells of "the New Jerusalem, a land of peace, a city of refuge, a place of safety for the saints of the Most High God" (D&C 45:66).

> And the glory of the Lord shall be there, and the terror of the Lord also shall be there, insomuch that the wicked will not come unto it, and it shall be called Zion. And it shall come to pass among the wicked, that every man that will not take his sword against his neighbor must needs flee unto Zion for safety. And there shall be gathered unto it out of every nation under heaven; and it shall be the only people that shall not be at war one with another. And it shall be said among the wicked: Let us not go up to battle against Zion, for the inhabitants of Zion are terrible; wherefore we cannot stand. And it shall come to pass that the righteous shall be gathered out from among all nations, and shall come to Zion, singing with songs of everlasting joy. (D&C 45:67–72; emphasis added.)

What I glean from this passage is that (1) there will be a city or land built up on earth in the last days called the New Jerusalem or Zion, (2) that if we don't "take up the sword" with our neighbors, we'll have to flee to this place, (3) Zion will be the only place on earth where the people will not be at war one with another, and (4) great dread will fill the wicked because the inhabitants of Zion will be indomitable. (I plan to focus on the New Jerusalem in a future post.)

Christ prophesied that in the last times, there would be "wars and rumours of wars" (see Matthew 24:6 and compare Mark 13:7).

And in that day shall be heard of wars and rumors of wars, and the whole earth shall be in commotion, and men's hearts shall fail them, and they shall say that Christ delayeth his coming until the end of the earth. (D&C 45:26).

Today we hear of wars and rumors of wars. These wars can consume our thoughts and make our hearts weary and perhaps fail. Luke tells us of a time when "upon the earth [there will be] distress of nations, with perplexity" (see Luke 21:25) and in modern scripture we read of "the wars and the perplexities of the nations" (D&C 88:79). Is this not our time?

I am reassured that we can "flee unto Zion for safety" now by gathering with the saints wherever they are, having genuine faith in Christ, repenting of our sins, living by the word of God rather than in fear of it, basking in the light of truth, cleansing our hearts, and becoming one, first with our families and then with those around and near us, for the Lord said, "Be one; and if ye are not one ye are not mine" (D&C 38:27).

And the Lord called his people Zion, because they were of one heart and one mind, and dwelt in righteousness; and there was no poor among them. (Moses 7:18.)

A fourth-century Christian bishop, Eusebius Pamphilus, wrote in his *Church History* (3.5.3) of the time when the early saints in Jerusalem were warned to flee the rebellious city before its destruction by Roman armies (66–70 AD):

> But the people of the church in Jerusalem had been commanded by a revelation, vouchsafed to approved men there before the war, to leave the city and to dwell in a certain town of Perea called Pella. And when those that believed in Christ had come there from Jerusalem, then, as if the royal city of the Jews and the whole land of Judea were entirely destitute of holy men, the judgment of God at length overtook those who had committed such outrages against Christ and his apostles, and totally destroyed that generation of impious men.

It is a time for us be wise. It is a time to be prepared. It is a time to set aside frivolous preoccupations. We were born in these times to stand up for the truth, and to stand by it in the midst of persecution and war.

In spite of fear and perplexity, we can rest assured that there will be a place of safety, and, even this very day, we can "stand in the holy place" (Matthew 24:15).

The scriptures tell of two witnesses who will prophesy in Jerusalem for two and half years just prior to the Second Coming of Jesus Christ.

# Chapter 17

# The Two Witnesses

The apostle John wrote about them in the book of Revelation:

> And I will give power unto my two witnesses, and they shall prophesy a thousand two hundred and threescore days, clothed in sackcloth. These are the two olive trees, and the two candlesticks standing before the God of the earth. (Revelation 11:3–4.)

Here is a brief summary of their ministry. Fire came out of the mouths of these prophets which destroyed their enemies. (That sounds like some kind of preaching. Wow.) They also shut up the heavens, causing a drought. After they were done bearing testimony in the city, power was given to the "beast" to kill them. While their bodies lay in the street, "people and kindreds and tongues and nations" rejoiced at their deaths and sent gifts to each other. (Could they see it on television or via the Internet?) After the three and a half days, the prophets rose from the dead and ascended into heaven, to the utter shock of their onlookers. Then there was a great earthquake and hail (see Revelation 11:5–12) which we've discussed in earlier posts.

The prophet Zechariah also prophesied of the "two olive trees":

> Then answered I, and said unto him, What are these two olive trees upon the right side of the candlestick and upon the left side thereof? And I answered again, and said unto him, What be these

two olive branches which through the two golden pipes empty the golden oil out of themselves? And he answered me and said, Knowest thou not what these be? And I said, No, my lord. Then said he, These are the two anointed ones, that stand by the Lord of the whole earth. (Zechariah 4:11–14; emphasis added.)

Isaiah also spoke of these two prophets:

These two things are come unto thee; who shall be sorry for thee? desolation, and destruction, and the famine, and the sword: by whom shall I comfort thee. Thy sons have fainted, they lie at the head of all the streets, as a wild bull in a net: they are full of the fury of the Lord, the rebuke of thy God. (Isaiah 51:19, 20; emphasis added.)

Modern revelation provides the following explanation:

Q. What is to be understood by the two witnesses, in the eleventh chapter of Revelation? A. They are two prophets that are to be raised up to the Jewish nation in the last days, at the time of the restoration, and to prophesy to the Jews after they are gathered and have built the city of Jerusalem in the land of their fathers. (D&C 77:15; emphasis added.)

The appearance of these prophets shows the pattern or law of witnesses:

In the mouth of tw no or three witnesses shall every word be established. (2 Corinthians 13:1.)

Two mighty prophets will prophesy in Jerusalem for several years before the coming of Christ. It appears that people across the globe will be aware of their ministry. They eventually will be killed but will in three days be resurrected and ascend into heaven. Not long after this will appear signs of the Second Coming of the Son of Man. What an incredible time this will be.

**Chapter 18**

# Gog and Magog, Armageddon, and the Valley of Jehoshaphat

The prophet Ezekiel tells of a great battle that will take place prior to the Second Coming of Christ. It is called the battle of Gog and Magog (see Ezekiel 38 and 39).

Gog is, as best we can tell, a gentile king of the land of Magog. The land of Magog is the land of Scythia which is near the Black Sea—modern Ukraine or southern Russia.

At the time of the Lord's coming, there will be "a great shaking" (or an earthquake) and the mountains will be "thrown down" and all walls will "fall to the ground" (see Ezekiel 38:19–20). There will also be a pestilence and an "overflowing rain":

> And I will plead against him with pestilence and with blood; and I will rain upon him, and upon his bands, and upon the many people that are with him, an overflowing rain, and great hailstones, fire, and brimstone. (Ezekiel 38:22.)

All this will take place in the valley of Jezreel. The valley of Jezreel is a large, fertile valley that lies southwest of the Sea of Galilee and northwest of Jerusalem. It is also called the valley of Megiddo because of hill or tell of Megiddo which overlooks it. (A tell is a location which becomes a hill due to many people inhabiting the same spot over long periods of time.) Interestingly, the city of Nazareth, the home of Jesus from his boyhood to early manhood, overlooks this valley.

We also read in the Bible Dictionary that the word Armageddon is:

> A Greek transliteration from the Hebrew Har Megiddon, or "Mountain of Megiddo." The valley of Megiddo is in the western portion of the plain of Esdraelon [Jezreel] about 75 miles north of Jerusalem. Several times the valley of Megiddo was the scene of violent and crucial battles during Old Testament times (Judges 5:19; 2 Kings 9:27; 23:29). A great and final conflict taking place at the Second Coming of the Lord is called the battle of Armageddon. See Zechariah [chapters] 11–14, especially Zechariah 12:11; Revelation 16:14–21. (Bible abbreviations expanded.)

The prophet Joel also mentions the valley of Jehoshaphat (also called the valley of decision), which lies between Jerusalem and the Mount of Olives to the east, in connection to this time:

> Let the heathen be wakened, and come up to the valley of Jehoshaphat: for there will I sit to judge all the heathen round about. Put ye in the sickle, for the harvest is ripe: come, get you down; for the press is full, the fats overflow; for their wickedness is great. Multitudes, multitudes in the valley of decision: for the day of the Lord is near in the valley of decision. (Joel 3:12–14; see also verse 2.)

Another battle called Gog and Magog, or the battle of the great God, will take place at the end of the Millennium when "the devil and his armies shall be cast away into their own place, that they shall not have power over the saints any more at all":

> And then he shall be loosed for a little season, that he may gather together his armies. And Michael,

the seventh angel, even the archangel, shall gather together his armies, even the hosts of heaven. And the devil shall gather together his armies; even the hosts of hell, and shall come up to battle against Michael and his armies. And then cometh the battle of the great God; and the devil and his armies shall be cast away into their own place, that they shall not have power over the saints any more at all. For Michael shall fight their battles, and shall overcome him who seeketh the throne of him who sitteth upon the throne, even the Lamb. This is the glory of God, and the sanctified; and they shall not any more see death. (D&C 88:111-116; see also Revelation 20:7–9.)

In conclusion, we learn from many sources that there will be a great battle prior to the coming of Christ that will take place in the valley of Jezreel and also in the valley of Jehoshaphat. This battle is commonly called the battle of Armageddon or the battle of Gog and Magog. It appears that this battle will end when Christ comes again, which will be punctuated, to put it lightly, with a great earthquake and a devastating storm. Another great battle, also called the battle of Gog and Magog, or the battle of the great God, will take place at the end of the Millennium, where the devil and his armies will be ultimately defeated for the last time.

# Chapter 19

# Whatsoever Nation Shall Possess This Land Shall Serve God or Be Swept Off

The Book of Mormon is a textbook for the latter days. Most everything that happened to the previous nations that possessed the lands that we now call North and South America will happen to us. One of the things that will happen is that the wicked will be swept from the land when the fulness of God's wrath will be visited upon them.

Near the end of the book, Moroni wrote these words as he related the history of the nation of the Jaredites from the Book of Ether:

> And he had sworn in his wrath unto the brother of Jared, that whoso should possess this land of promise, from that time henceforth and forever, should serve him, the true and only God, or they should be swept off when the fulness of his wrath should come upon them. And now, we can behold the decrees of God concerning this land, that it is a land of promise; and whatsoever nation shall possess it shall serve God, or they shall be swept off when the fulness of his wrath shall come upon them. And the fulness of his wrath cometh upon them when they are ripened in iniquity. For behold, this is a land which is choice above all other lands; wherefore he that doth possess it shall serve God or shall be swept off; for it is the everlasting decree of God. And it is not until the

fulness of iniquity among the children of the land, that they are swept off. (Ether 2:8–10; emphasis added.)

This seems to apply to any land of promise. For example, when Jerusalem fell into spiritual ruin, the Babylonians (pictured above; see 2 Kings 24, 25) and the Romans destroyed and flattened the city. In the Book of Mormon, insuperable destruction swept the land of wicked inhabitants at the time of the Jaredites, at the time of Christ's death, and when the Nephites were destroyed by the Lamanites in the early centuries after Christ appeared in America.

I wish to say that there is a difference between the wicked and the righteous. Given the political rhetoric of our day, sometimes we hear evil called good and good called evil (see Isaiah 5:20), but rest assured that there will be a day that will burn as an oven where all the proud and wicked will be as dry stubble in the field and the righteous "shall tread down the wicked; for they shall be ashes under the soles of [their] feet" (see Malachi 4:1, 3).

We seem to live in the midst of a cyclone of iniquity. The storm could quiet through repentance, through the acceptance of God's existence and laws, but such will not be the case. Not in this era.

# Chapter 20

# The Same Day Lot Went Out of Sodom It Rained Fire and Brimstone

Sometime before His Olivet discourse, which He gave only days before His death, the Savior prophesied of His Second Coming in Luke chapter 17:

And as it was in the days of Noe, so shall it be also in the days of the Son of man. They did eat, they drank, they married wives, they were given in marriage, until the day that Noe entered into the ark, and the flood came, and destroyed them all. Likewise also as it was in the days of Lot; they did eat, they drank, they bought, they sold, they planted, they builded; but the same day that Lot went out of Sodom it rained fire and brimstone from heaven, and destroyed them all. Even thus shall it be in the day when the Son of man is revealed. (Luke 17:26–30; emphasis added.)

As it was in the days of Noah, as it was in the days of Lot, so will it be when the Son of God returns again to earth. It seems that day will be a scene of sudden, mass destruction. Why? I'll explore what happened to Lot and his family. It'll give us an idea of what might happen on the "great and dreadful day of the Lord" (Malachi 4:5).

Before Sodom was destroyed, Abraham and Lot, Abraham's nephew, lived near Bethel and Ai, probably about 15 to 20 miles (24 to 32 kilometers) north of Jerusalem. Between them they owned a lot of livestock and they couldn't live near each other without their herdsmen arguing, so Lot and his family departed to the east, to the fertile, alluvial plain near the city of Sodom. This area was likely just northeast of the Dead Sea (also called the Salt Sea).

Lot was in for a little trouble though because "the men of Sodom were wicked and sinners before the Lord exceedingly" (Genesis 13:13).

In time, holy men came to Abraham and Sarah to tell them of the birth of Isaac, and as the men departed, the Lord revealed his intentions for Sodom to Abraham:

> And the Lord said, Because *the cry of Sodom and Gomorrah is great, and because their sin is very grievous*; I will go down now, and see whether they have done altogether according to the cry of it, which is come unto me; and if not, I will know. (Genesis 18:20–21; emphasis added.)

Abraham reasoned with the Lord, pleading that He spare the cities if only ten righteous people were there. The Lord promised that He would not destroy them for the sake of ten. Nevertheless, in the end, the cities were not spared.

When two angels arrived in Sodom, they stayed in Lot's house. I'll rely on the New International Version to tell us clearly what happened next.

> Before they had gone to bed, all the men from every part of the city of Sodom—both young and old—surrounded the house. They called to Lot, "Where are the men who came to you tonight? Bring them out to us so that we can have sex with them." Lot went outside to meet them and shut the door behind him and said, "No, my friends. Don't do this wicked thing. . . . [can't bear to leave in the part about Lot's daughters] Don't do anything to these men, for they have come under the protection of my roof."

"Get out of our way," they replied. "This fellow came here as a foreigner, and now he wants to play the judge! We'll treat you worse than them." They kept bringing pressure on Lot and moved forward to break down the door. But the men inside reached out and pulled Lot back into the house and shut the door. Then they struck the men who were at the door of the house, young and old, with blindness so that they could not find the door. (NIV Genesis 19:4–11.)

Jude, who was likely Jesus's younger brother, wrote in his epistle that:

> Sodom and Gomorrah and the surrounding towns gave themselves up to sexual immorality and perversion. They serve as an example of those who suffer the punishment of eternal fire. (NIV Jude 1:7.)

But immorality and perversion weren't Sodom's only sins. The Lord also condemned Jerusalem by the mouth of Ezekiel the prophet, comparing her to Sodom:

> Thy younger sister, that dwelleth at thy right hand, is Sodom and her daughters. Yet hast thou not walked after their ways, nor done after their abominations: but, as if that were a very little thing, thou wast corrupted more than they in all thy ways. As I live, saith the Lord God, Sodom thy sister hath not done, she nor her daughters, as thou hast done, thou and thy daughters. Behold, this was the iniquity of thy sister Sodom, pride, fulness of bread [overeating], and abundance of idleness [unconcerned, perhaps lazy or apathetic] was in her and in her daughters, neither did she strengthen the hand of the poor and needy. And they were haughty, and committed abomination

before me: therefore I took them away as I saw good. (Ezekiel 16:46–50; emphasis added.)

Lot tried to warn his sons in law, but they thought he was full of beans. When Lot lingered the next morning, the angels took Lot and his family by the hand and ("set") them outside the walls of the city. After they entered the nearby village of Zoar (Bela), "the Lord rained upon Sodom and upon Gomorrah brimstone and fire from the Lord out of heaven; and he overthrew those cities, and all the plain, and all the inhabitants of the cities, and that which grew upon the ground" (Genesis 19:23–25).

When Lot's wife looked back at the destruction, which she had been forbidden to do, she was reduced to a pillar of salt.

In his testimony to His disciples, Jesus warned: "Remember Lot's wife." What should we remember about her? Against the counsel of angels, she looked back. She chose her own way and suffered the fate of those who remained in the city.

I don't know precisely what happened to Lot's wife, but I have a suspicion that she not only looked back, she actually turned back and placed herself within the sulfuric strike zone. What was she after? I don't know. But this we do know: she brought her punishment upon herself. (Jeffrey R. Holland gave a wonderful devotional at BYU entitled "Remember Lot's Wife." Recommended reading.)

Heed the warnings of the holy prophets, warn others to flee from sin, flee from sin ourselves, and don't look back.

**Note:** The archeologist Steven Collins believes that Tall el-Hammam, just northeast of the Dead Sea, is a geographical and archeological match for the site of ancient Sodom. He has been excavating the tell since 2005 and has discovered a thick layer of ash and other evidence that the city was exposed to a sudden, intense heat reaching 2,000 degrees Fahrenheit. After the city was destroyed, the location was uninhabited for some 700 years. We can't be certain that Tall el-Hammam is the same place as Sodom as there are arguments against it, but I believe it might just be the place.

# Chapter 21

# A Thief in the Night

The Second Coming of Christ will take many by surprise. It will come as a "thief in the night," as the apostle Peter says in his second epistle:

> But the day of the Lord will come as a thief in the night; in the which the heavens shall pass away with a great noise, and the elements shall melt with fervent heat, the earth also and the works that are therein shall be burned up. (2 Peter 3:10; see also 1 Thessalonians 5:2; emphasis added.)

Modern revelation reaffirms the simile:

> And again, verily I say unto you, the coming of the Lord draweth nigh, and it overtaketh the world as a thief in the night—therefore, gird up your loins, that you may be the children of light, and that day shall not overtake you as a thief. (D&C 106:4–5; compare D&C 45:19; emphasis added.)

Here we learn that the Second Coming will not only surprise the world; it will also overtake it. The Lord himself says:

> Behold, I come as a thief. Blessed is he that watcheth, and keepeth his garments, lest he walk naked, and they see his shame. (Revelation 16:15; emphasis added.)

Let's think about this literary image of a thief for a moment. I want to talk about three things: (1) surprise, (2) sleep, and (3) stealing. First, the surprise. Everyone on this planet will both see and hear the sign of the coming of the Son of Man. For example, we read in Luke:

> For as the lightning, that lighteneth out of the one part under heaven, shineth unto the other part under heaven; so shall also the Son of man be in his day. (Luke 17:24.)

And in the Doctrine and Covenants:

> And another angel shall sound his trump, saying: That great church, the mother of abominations . . . she is ready to be burned. And he shall sound his trump both long and loud, and all nations shall hear it. (D&C 88:94; emphasis added.)

Everyone will see the light and hear the sound of the trumpet. Most will not be ready. Dread and fear will overtake those who are not ready for that day. But to those who are ready, I think the surprise will be something like Christmas morning: you know the day is coming; you prepare for it as well as you can; but you are not exactly sure what you are going to get. It will be a truly wonderful day for those who are prepared, surprise notwithstanding.

Second, sleep. When a thief comes at night, his victims are usually sleeping. When the Lord comes again, many in the world will be spiritually asleep or spiritually distracted, like the evil servant in Jesus' Olivet discourse:

> But and if that evil servant shall say in his heart, My lord delayeth his coming; and shall begin to smite his fellowservants, and to eat and drink with the drunken; the lord of that servant shall come in a day when he looketh not for him, and in an hour that he is not aware of, and shall cut him asunder, and appoint him his portion with the hypocrites:

there shall be weeping and gnashing of teeth.
(Matthew 24:48–51; emphasis added.)

That will be an embarrassing, devastating moment.
Let's not "eat and drink with the drunken."

Finally, stealing. What might "the thief in the night"
steal from those he overtakes? Their illusions and their
false sense of security, and their over-dependence on
intellectual assumptions and material wealth. Gulp.

Let us be the children of light so that the thief will not
overtake us (see D&C 106:5).

# Chapter 22

# The Sun Shall Be Darkened

One prophecy about the time leading up to the Second Coming that appears again and again is a sign from the heavens. Isaiah mentions it:

> For the stars of heaven and the constellations thereof shall not give their light: the sun shall be darkened in his going forth, and the moon shall not cause her light to shine. (Isaiah 13:10; compare Isaiah 24:23.)

As does the prophet Joel:

> The earth shall quake before them; the heavens shall tremble: the sun and the moon shall be dark, and the stars shall withdraw their shining . . . . The sun shall be turned into darkness, and the moon into blood, before the great and the terrible day of the Lord come. (Joel 2:10,31; see also Joel 3:15.)

Ezekiel also adds:

> And when I shall put thee out, I will cover the heaven, and make the stars thereof dark; I will cover the sun with a cloud, and the moon shall not give her light. All the bright lights of heaven will I make dark over thee, and set darkness upon thy land, saith the Lord God. (Ezekiel 32:7–8.)

The Savior also spoke of this prophecy just days before His crucifixion, death, and resurrection:

> Immediately after the tribulation of those days shall the sun be darkened, and the moon shall not give her light, and the stars shall fall from heaven,

and the powers of the heavens shall be shaken. (Matthew 24:29; compare Mark 13:24–25 and Luke 21:25.)

And modern scripture repeats the refrain:

But, behold, I say unto you that before this great day shall come the sun shall be darkened, and the moon shall be turned into blood, and the stars shall fall from heaven, and there shall be greater signs in heaven above and in the earth beneath. (D&C 29:14; compare D&C 34:9 and D&C 88:87.)

There are several things that come to mind readily that could contribute to this phenomena. For example, the sun and moon could be obscured by smoke from a fire or there could be a solar or lunar eclipse.

If we dig a little deeper, though, it appears that this sign will actually accompany the Lord's coming. Section 133 of the Doctrine and Covenants sheds this additional, compelling light:

And so great shall be the glory of his presence that the sun shall hide his face in shame, and the moon shall withhold its light, and the stars shall be hurled from their places. (D&C 133:49.)

This verse indicates that it will be the glory of His presence that will obscure the light of these orbs, that He himself will eclipse the light of the sun and moon, and hurl the stars around the sky. This seems quite fitting when we remember that another heavenly sign: a new star appeared when He was born (see, for example, Matthew 2:2, 9, 10, Helaman 14:1–7, and 3 Nephi 1:15–19).

In conclusion, the prophet Micah adds this spiritual insight:

> Therefore night shall be unto you, that ye shall not
> have a vision; and it shall be dark unto you, that ye
> shall not divine; and the sun shall go down over
> the prophets, and the day shall be dark over them.
> (Micah 3:6.)

Once again, we can only speculate on exactly how these things will manifest themselves, but if we continue to prayerfully study the scriptures, we'll be better prepared to grasp these heavenly signs when they actually happen.

# Chapter 23

# At Evening Time It Shall Be Light

When Christ comes again, there will be an incredible sign in the heavens, something like a magnificent sunrise.

Wherefore if they shall say unto you, Behold, he is in the desert; go not forth: behold, he is in the secret chambers; believe it not. For as the lightning cometh out of the east, and shineth even unto the west; so shall also the coming of the Son of man be. (Matthew 24:26–27; compare Joseph Smith—Matthew 1:25–26.)

Remember that at His first coming, at His birth, the light remained bright throughout the night, as we read in 3 Nephi:

And it came to pass that the words which came unto Nephi were fulfilled, according as they had been spoken; for behold, at the going down of the sun there was no darkness; and the people began to be astonished because there was no darkness when the night came . . . . And it came to pass that there was no darkness in all that night, but it was as light as though it was mid-day. And it came to pass that the sun did rise in the morning again, according to its proper order; and they knew that it was the day that the Lord should be born, because of the sign which had been given. (3 Nephi 1:15, 19.)

Zechariah prophesied that the same thing will happen when Christ comes a second time. In chapter 14, he tells us that when "the day of the Lord cometh" (verse 1), after His feet shall stand on the mount of Olives (verse 4), that a similar sign will be manifest:

And it shall come to pass in that day, that the light shall not be clear, nor dark: but it shall be one day which shall be known to the Lord, not day, nor night: but it shall come to pass, that at evening time it shall be light. (Zechariah 14:6–7.)

Isaiah tells us in yet another prophesy of the Lord's coming that there will be at that time a remarkable light.

Moreover the light of the moon shall be as the light of the sun, and the light of the sun shall be sevenfold, as the light of seven days, in the day that the Lord bindeth up the breach of his people, and healeth the stroke of their wound. (Isaiah 30:26.)

That night will be a celebration for the victory of our Lord over all wickedness. Evil will be vanquished at the presence of His light, and whether I am in a mortal or immortal state, I plan to stay up all night partying. I hope to see you there!

Finally—and I plan to write more about this in upcoming posts—let's remember that after the millennial day, when the earth becomes a celestial sphere, the new Jerusalem will descend again to earth (see Revelation 21:2, 10) and Christ Himself will be the light of that city:

And the city had no need of the sun, neither of the moon, to shine in it: for the glory of God did lighten it, and the Lamb is the light thereof. And the nations of them which are saved shall walk in the light of it: and the kings of the earth do bring their glory and honour into it. (Revelation 21:23–24.)

# Chapter 24

# Silence in Heaven for the Space of Half an Hour

An interesting phenomena will occur very near the time of Christ's coming. It's mentioned several times in the scriptures. I like the clarity of the passage in the Doctrine and Covenants:

> And there shall be silence in heaven for the space of half an hour; and immediately after shall the curtain of heaven be unfolded, as a scroll is unfolded after it is rolled up, and the face of the Lord shall be unveiled. (D&C 88:95.)

The apostle John also tells us:

> And when he had opened the seventh seal, there was silence in heaven about the space of half an hour. (Revelation 8:1.)

Seven angels blowing seven trumpets are also mentioned in these passages, each announcing wonders on the earth (D&C 88:93–107; see also Revelation 8:2–10:11.)

I will cover the seven angels and the seven trumpets in the next chapter; here I only want to discuss the silence in heaven.

The Doctrine and Covenants says that there will be "a great sign in heaven" (D&C 88:93) and we will hear the first angel declare:

> And another angel shall sound his trump, saying: That great church, the mother of abominations,

that made all nations drink of the wine of the wrath of her fornication, that persecuteth the saints of God, that shed their blood—she who sitteth upon many waters, and upon the islands of the sea—behold, she is the tares of the earth; she is bound in bundles; her bands are made strong, no man can loose them; therefore, she is ready to be burned. And he shall sound his trump both long and loud, and all nations shall hear it. (D&C 88:94; emphasis added.)

A haunting image. Imagine hearing this devastating indictment pronounced on the world, followed by the long, loud sound of a trumpet that everyone hears. Everyone hears it! Then a spine-tingling half hour of silence.

What will we be thinking during that half hour? What will we be feeling? Astonishment? Anticipation? Fear? Dread? Horror? Excitement? Vindication? Exultation?

Who will you call on your cell phone? Will the airwaves be jammed?

Will you pace or fidget? Will you look up or down? Will you run and hide?

And they shall go into the holes of the rocks, and into the caves of the earth, for fear of the Lord, and for the glory of his majesty, when he ariseth to shake terribly the earth. In that day a man shall cast his idols of silver, and his idols of gold, which they made each one for himself to worship, to the [blind] moles and to the [blind] bats; to go into the clefts of the rocks, and into the tops of the ragged rocks, for fear of the Lord, and for the glory of his majesty, when he ariseth to shake terribly the earth. (Isaiah 2:19–21.)

Truly, "every ear shall hear it, and every knee shall bow, and every tongue shall confess" (D&C 88:104). There will be no hiding. It truly will be a remarkable moment.

# Chapter 25

# Angels Sounding the Trump of God

At or just before His Second Coming, seven angels will sound the trump of God to the inhabitants of the earth, preparing them for the appearance of Jesus Christ. All nations on earth will hear these startling messages of judgment and destruction (D&C 88:94) and "fear shall come upon all people" (D&C 88:91).

Seven is a sacred number representing perfection or completeness. These angels will have a lot to say and do to finish their work of preparation. Following is a recap of some of their messages as recorded in the Book of Revelation, chapter 8 through 18 and in the Doctrine and Covenants chapter 88 verses 87 through 116.

In the Book of Revelation, beginning in chapter 8, John writes of "seven angels which had the seven trumpets [who] prepared themselves to sound" (Revelation 8:6). This chapter reveals that these angels will bring destruction to the earth:

• "The first angel sounded, and there followed hail and fire mingled with blood, and they were cast upon the earth: and the third part of trees was burnt up, and all green grass was burnt up" (v. 7).

• "And the second angel sounded, and as it were a great mountain burning with fire was cast into the sea: and the third part of the sea became blood; and the third part of the creatures which were in the sea, and had life, died; and the third part of the ships were destroyed" (v. 8–9; compare 16:3).

• "And the third angel sounded, and there fell a great star from heaven, burning as it were a lamp, and it fell upon the third part of the rivers, and upon the fountains of waters; and the name of the star is called Wormwood: and the third part of the waters became wormwood; and many men died of the waters, because they were made bitter" (v. 10–11; compare 16:4–7).

• "And the fourth angel sounded, and the third part of the sun was smitten, and the third part of the moon, and the third part of the stars; so as the third part of them was darkened, and the day shone not for a third part of it, and the night likewise" (v. 12; compare 16:8–9).

The first 12 verses of chapter 9 speaks of the fifth angel who has the key to the bottomless pit and who will send forth and hurt "those men which have not the seal of God in their foreheads" (v. 4; compare 16:10–11). Verses 13 through 31 talk of the sixth angel. If my math is right, this angel foretells the appearance of 200,000,000 mounted horsemen—when or where was there ever an army to compare—who go forth to destroy many of those who will not repent. (See also chapter 16:12–16).

In chapter 10 of Revelation, the seventh angel (v. 7) comes down from heaven (v. 1) and "in his hand [he has] a little book open: and he set his right foot upon the sea, and his left foot on the earth, and cried with a loud voice, as when a lion roareth: and when he had cried, seven thunders uttered their voices" (v. 2–3). John was forbidden to write what the seven thunders uttered but upon ingesting the little book in the angel's hand was promised that he would yet prophesy "before many peoples, and nations, and tongues, and kings (v. 11). (See also chapter 16:17–21).

Then again, in the 14th chapter of Revelation, we read of "another angel fly[ing] in the midst of heaven, having the everlasting gospel to preach unto them that dwell on the earth, and to every nation, and kindred, and tongue, and people, saying with a loud voice, Fear God, and give glory to him; for the hour of his judgment is come: and worship him that made heaven, and earth, and the sea, and the fountains of waters" (Revelation 14:6–7).

Then another angel speaks saying, "Babylon is fallen, is fallen, that great city, because she made all nations drink of the wine of the wrath of her fornication" (v. 8). Then the third angel speaks: "If any man worship the beast and his image, and receive his mark in his forehead, or in his hand, The same shall drink of the wine of the wrath of God, which is poured out without mixture into the cup of his indignation; and he shall be tormented with fire and brimstone in the presence of the holy angels, and in the presence of the Lamb . . ." (v. 9–11). And several others followed, one saying: "Thrust in thy sickle, and reap: for the time is come for thee to reap; for the harvest of the earth is ripe" (v. 15–20).

In Revelation 15, John tells us that the seven angels will pour out the last plagues on the earth.

> And the seven angels came out of the temple, having the seven plagues, clothed in pure and white linen, and having their breasts girded with golden girdles. And one of the four beasts gave unto the seven angels seven golden vials full of the wrath of God, who liveth for ever and ever. And the temple was filled with smoke from the glory of God, and from his power; and no man was able to enter into the temple, till the seven plagues of the seven angels were fulfilled. (Revelation 15:6–8.)

Chapter 16 recounts the plagues and their effect on those who "repented not of their deeds" (v. 11).

Doctrine and Covenants 88:92–106: also speaks of seven angels, angels crying with a loud voice: "Prepare ye, prepare ye, O inhabitants of the earth; for the judgment of our God is come. Behold, and lo, the Bridegroom cometh; go ye out to meet him" (v. 92).

• Though not named, the first angel will sound with these words: "That great church, the mother of abominations, that made all nations drink of the wine of the wrath of her fornication, that persecuteth the saints of God, that shed their blood—she who sitteth upon many waters, and upon the islands of the sea—behold, she is the tares of the earth; she is bound in bundles; her bands are made strong, no man can loose them; therefore, she is ready to be burned" (v. 94; compare Revelation 17).

• The second angel: "Then cometh the redemption of those who are Christ's at his coming; who have received their part in that prison which is prepared for them, that they might receive the gospel, and be judged according to men in the flesh" (v. 99).

• The third angel: "Then come the spirits of men who are to be judged, and are found under condemnation; and these are the rest of the dead; and they live not again until the thousand years are ended, neither again, until the end of the earth" (v. 100–101).

• The fourth angel: "There are found among those who are to remain until that great and last day, even the end, who shall remain filthy still" (v. 102).

• The fifth angel: "Committeth the everlasting gospel— flying through the midst of heaven, unto all nations, kindreds, tongues, and people; and this shall be the sound of his trump, saying to all people, both in heaven and in earth, and that are under the earth—for every ear shall hear it, and every knee shall bow, and every tongue shall confess, while they hear the sound of the trump, saying: Fear God, and give glory to him who sitteth upon the throne, forever and ever; for the hour of his judgment is come" (v. 103–104; compare Revelation 14:6–7).

• The sixth angel: "She is fallen who made all nations drink of the wine of the wrath of her fornication; she is fallen, is fallen!" (v. 105).

• Finally, the seventh angel: "It is finished; it is finished! The Lamb of God hath overcome and trodden the wine-press alone, even the wine-press of the fierceness of the wrath of Almighty God" (v. 106; compare Revelation 16:17).

Then the first through the seventh angels shall sound again, revealing "the secret acts of men, and the mighty works of God" during the first through the seventh thousand-year periods (see D&C 88:108–110).

What are we to learn from these accounts? That God will send seven angels at or near Christ's coming and these angels will both pronounce and execute secret acts, woes, judgments, and destructions that will come upon the earth at the time of Christ's Second Coming and also, it seems, at the end of the temporal world, which will occur after the Millennium.

To the faithful, the trump of angels will be welcome, glorious, and joyous; for those who are not faithful, no so much.

## Chapter 26

# The Lord Shall Be Red in His Apparel

When I think about the Savior, I usually think of His love, of the goodness and mercy He shows us "according to the multitude of his lovingkindnesses" (Isaiah 63:7). But that won't be the case at His Second Coming, not for His enemies anyway. To them, that day will be a day of vengeance.

Do you suppose you can get rid of the justice of an offended God?

> And wo be unto him that will not hearken unto the words of Jesus, and also to them whom he hath chosen and sent among them; for whoso receiveth not the words of Jesus and the words of those whom he hath sent receiveth not him; and therefore he will not receive them at the last day; and it would be better for them if they had not been born. For do ye suppose that ye can get rid of the justice of an offended God, who hath been trampled under feet of men, that thereby salvation might come? (3 Nephi 28:34–35.)

Accordingly, when Jesus comes again, He will not be dressed in white. He will be dressed in red—blood red. John the Revelator wrote:

And he was clothed with a vesture dipped in blood: and his name is called The Word of God. And the armies which were in heaven followed him upon white horses, clothed in fine linen, white and clean. (Revelation 19:13–14; emphasis added.)

Modern revelation echoes John's vision, as do the writings of Isaiah:

> O Lord, thou shalt come down to make thy name known to thine adversaries, and all nations shall tremble at thy presence— . . . And it shall be said: Who is this that cometh down from God in heaven with dyed garments; yea, from the regions which are not known, clothed in his glorious apparel, traveling in the greatness of his strength? And he shall say: I am he who spake in righteousness, mighty to save. And the Lord shall be red in his apparel, and his garments like him that treadeth in the wine-vat. (D&C 133:42, 46–48; emphasis added.)

And why will be He be dressed in red?

> And his voice shall be heard: I have trodden the wine-press alone, and have brought judgment upon all people; and none were with me; and I have trampled them in my fury, and I did tread upon them in mine anger, and their blood have I sprinkled upon my garments, and stained all my raiment; for this was the day of vengeance which was in my heart. (D&C 133:50–51; compare Isaiah 63:1-7; emphasis added.)

When I see the uncountable and unaccountable crimes, the sickening atrocities, the abominations, the injustices, the ornate selfishness, the cruel covetousness, and the downright wickedness of this badly off-balance world— and to be sure this wickedness has continued since the day Cain slew Abel until now—I admit I am anxious for the winding up scene, but I know I must be patient.

Wait on the Lord: be of good courage, and he shall strengthen thine heart: wait, I say, on the Lord. (Psalms 27:14.)

I am not anxious to condemn the weak, the discouraged, or the repenting sinner, for I am among them. I am not disposed to condemn anyone. But of those who worship Satan, those who serve the devil, his devotees, perhaps unknowingly, John also wrote:

> The third angel followed them, saying with a loud voice, If any man worship the beast and his image, and receive his mark in his forehead, or in his hand, the same shall drink of the wine of the wrath of God, which is poured out without mixture into the cup of his indignation; and he shall be tormented with fire and brimstone in the presence of the holy angels, and in the presence of the Lamb. (Revelation 19:9–10; emphasis added.)

Woes await the unflinching and determinedly wicked. We need not be among them.

I admit that I must strive daily for mastery over the natural man (see 2 Timothy 2:5), but I don't do it out of fear. I do it out of reverence, for God our Heavenly Father, for what is right and good and holy, and for His Son our Savior, whose coming I cherish.

# Chapter 27

# Caught Up to Meet Him

At Christ's Second Coming, faithful saints, both those on earth as mortals and those in their graves, will be caught up to meet him in the clouds. What is the so-called "rapture" and when will it take place?

We know that Jesus will not be alone when He comes. Jude, the Lord's brother, quotes Enoch, telling us that Jesus "cometh with ten thousands of his saints" (see Jude 1:14; compare 1 Thessalonians 3:13).

The traditional Christian source text for the "rapture" is found in 1 Thessalonians:

> For if we believe that Jesus died and rose again, even so them also which sleep in Jesus will God bring with him. For this we say unto you by the word of the Lord, that we which are alive and remain unto the coming of the Lord shall not prevent [precede] them which are asleep. For the Lord himself shall descend from heaven with a shout, with the voice of the archangel, and with the trump of God: and the dead in Christ shall rise first: then we which are alive and remain shall be caught up together with them in the clouds, to meet the Lord in the air: and so shall we ever be with the Lord. Wherefore comfort one another with these words. (1 Thessalonians 4:14–17; emphasis added.)

It appears that the time of being "caught up . . . in the clouds" will take place at the same time that Christ actually comes. He hinted at this dramatic time in His Olivet discourse when He said:

> Then shall two be in the field; the one shall be taken, and the other left. Two women shall be grinding at the mill; the one shall be taken, and the other left. (Matthew 24:40–41; emphasis added.)

Modern revelation also speaks of this amazing day:

> And the saints that are upon the earth, who are alive, shall be quickened and be caught up to meet him. And they who have slept in their graves shall come forth, for their graves shall be opened; and they also shall be caught up to meet him in the midst of the pillar of heaven—they are Christ's, the first fruits, they who shall descend with him first, and they who are on the earth and in their graves, who are first caught up to meet him; and all this by the voice of the sounding of the trump of the angel of God. (D&C 88:96–98; compare D&C 109:75; see also D&C 78:20–21; emphasis added.)

So when Christ comes again, He will come with thousands of saints and will be joined by thousands of saints who are yet mortal or who have not yet been resurrected. Those who will be resurrected at this time will be "first caught up to meet him."

What a spectacular moment that will be. But an even more important moment is this moment. What can we do, you and I, right now at this moment to better prepare ourselves for the great and dreadful day (see Malachi 4:5)?

# Chapter 28

# Calamity Shall Cover the Mocker

The Broadway musical "The Book of Mormon," created by the South Park duo Parker and Stone, mocks Latter-day Saints, their faith and religion, their missionaries and culture, in a vulgar and absurd way.

Don't get me wrong. Mormons have a funny, sometimes endearing, sometimes hilarious culture with plenty to tickle the ribs. I am sure we can look pretty odd to others as we attempt to live our faith. With family and friends, I've had my share of laughs at myself and the quirky culture that swirls around us.

But mocking is different. To mock is to criticize, laugh at, or make fun of. It belittles, puts down, and plays down. It distorts and deceives. It separates people. It's rude and unkind and often heartless. It's a pernicious form of propaganda. It invites clashes and conflict and sometimes violence.

I've often wondered, since it came out in 2011, how the musical might have been received if the producers chose Muslims instead of Mormons to make fun of. I suppose some rights should be valued above the right of free speech, such as the right to life itself.

In the end, this Broadway venture will not endure the test of time. In time, it will be "thrust down" like every other unholy thing. As the Lord told Moroni, "fools mock, but they shall mourn" (see Ether 12:28).

Jude, who is thought to be a brother of Jesus and James, wrote that:

There should be mockers in the last time, who should walk after their own ungodly lusts. These be they who separate themselves, sensual, having not the Spirit. (Jude 1:18–19.)

Nephi spoke of those who pointed their fingers and mocked from the "great and spacious building":

And I also cast my eyes round about, and beheld, on the other side of the river of water, a great and spacious building; and it stood as it were in the air, high above the earth. And it was filled with people, both old and young, both male and female; and their manner of dress was exceedingly fine; and they were in the attitude of mocking and pointing their fingers towards those who had come at and were partaking of the fruit [of the tree of life]. (1 Nephi 8:26–27.)

Before the destruction of Jerusalem and its temple at the hands of Babylonian invaders, we read:

Moreover all the chief of the priests, and the people, transgressed very much after all the abominations of the heathen; and polluted the house of the Lord which he had hallowed in Jerusalem. And the Lord God of their fathers sent to them by his messengers, rising up betimes, and sending; because he had compassion on his people, and on his dwelling place: but they mocked the messengers of God, and despised his words, and misused his prophets, until the wrath of the Lord arose against his people, till there was no remedy. (2 Chronicles 36:14–16.)

Finally, at the time of Christ's Second Coming, we also read that "calamity shall cover the mocker":

And the Lord shall utter his voice, and all the ends of the earth shall hear it; and the nations of the earth shall mourn, and they that have laughed shall see their folly. And calamity shall cover the mocker, and the scorner shall be consumed; and they that have watched for iniquity shall be hewn down and cast into the fire. (D&C 45:49–50.)

I don't intend to mock the mockers here. I don't want to mock anyone. I just want to point out that if you or I mock what is good and right and pure, it will not go well for us.

Be not deceived; God is not mocked: for whatsoever a man soweth, that shall he also reap. (Galatians 6:7.)

I take the same advice that I offer: Be careful what you say about sacred things.

# Chapter 29

# The Day Cometh that Shall Burn As an Oven

Just as a flood destroyed the earth and its inhabitants in Noah's day (see Genesis 7), prophets have told us that the earth will be destroyed by fire in a future day. Perhaps not far in the future.

This is not happy news. It's a terrifying prospect, really. Incomprehensible, a disaster of epic proportion. But it is well attested in scripture. And because it comes from scripture, it's not just a possibility and it's more than probability. It's a prophecy, and, soon or late, prophecy comes to pass.

In the last book of the Old Testament, we read an important question:

> But who may abide the day of his coming? and who shall stand when he appeareth? for he is like a refiner's fire, and like fullers' soap: and he shall sit as a refiner and purifier of silver: and he shall purify the sons of Levi, and purge them as gold and silver, that they may offer unto the Lord an offering in righteousness. Then shall the offering of Judah and Jerusalem be pleasant unto the Lord, as in the days of old, and as in former years. (Malachi 3:2–4.)

How will He be like a refiner's fire? Isaiah spoke of a time in the last days when the earth would be defiled by sin and the inhabitants burned:

The earth also is defiled under the inhabitants thereof; because they have transgressed the laws, changed the ordinance, broken the everlasting covenant. Therefore hath the curse devoured the earth, and they that dwell therein are desolate: therefore the inhabitants of the earth are burned, and few men left. (Isaiah 24:5–6; emphasis added.)

Malachi's well-known prophecy about the burning of the earth tells us that the wicked will be as stubble, as the fields after harvest:

For, behold, the day cometh, that shall burn as an oven; and all the proud, yea, and all that do wickedly, shall be stubble: and the day that cometh shall burn them up, saith the Lord of hosts, that it shall leave them neither root nor branch. (Malachi 4:1; compare D&C 29:9; D&C 64:24; and D&C 133:64.)

The apostle Peter wrote in his second epistle that the earth and the wicked works therein will be burned up:

But the day of the Lord will come as a thief in the night; in the which the heavens shall pass away with a great noise, and the elements shall melt with fervent heat, the earth also and the works that are therein shall be burned up. (2 Peter 3:10.)

How will the earth be burned? The prophet Nahum tells us that the earth will be burned at the presence of the Lord.

The mountains quake at him, and the hills melt, and the earth is burned at his presence, yea, the world, and all that dwell therein. (Nahum 1:5; emphasis added.)

Modern revelation also testifies that the presence of the Lord will be as a "fire that burneth":

> And it shall be answered upon their heads; for the presence of the Lord shall be as the melting fire that burneth, and as the fire which causeth the waters to boil. (D&C 133:41; see also D&C 88:94; emphasis added.)

And another place the Doctrine and Covenants says:

> And the saints also shall hardly escape; nevertheless, I, the Lord, am with them, and will come down in heaven from the presence of my Father and consume the wicked with unquenchable fire. (D&C 63:34; emphasis added.)

How is He like a refiner's fire? Perhaps because the light and power of His presence will have a purifying effect on the righteous and a destructive effect on the wicked.

Nephi tells us that the fire will actually be a protection to the righteous:

> Wherefore, he will preserve the righteous by his power, even if it so be that the fulness of his wrath must come, and the righteous be preserved, even unto the destruction of their enemies by fire. Wherefore, the righteous need not fear; for thus saith the prophet, they shall be saved, even if it so be as by fire. (1 Nephi 22:17; see also vs. 22–23.)

Finally, the Lord's protection will be effective:

> And ye shall tread down the wicked; for they shall be ashes under the soles of your feet in the day that I shall do this, saith the Lord of hosts. (Malachi 4:3.)

When the saints, living and dead, are "caught up together
. . . to meet the Lord in the air" (see 1 Thessalonians
4:17), they will be protected from the destruction that
will take place on earth. How the two events go together,
I am not sure. But I think they do go together.

# Chapter 30

# The New Jerusalem

When He visited the Nephites in the New World, the Savior told them that He would establish His people in a place called the New Jerusalem, and that the city would established "in this land":

> And behold, this people will I establish in this land, unto the fulfilling of the covenant which I made with your father Jacob; and it shall be a New Jerusalem. And the powers of heaven shall be in the midst of this people; yea, even I will be in the midst of you. (3 Nephi 20:22; see also 3 Nephi 21:22–25.)

Where is "this land"? We know from modern revelation that the city of New Jerusalem or Zion will be established in the last days on the American continent (see Articles of Faith 1:10). In the Book of Mormon, Moroni spoke of the ancient writings of Ether on the subject (see Ether 13:1–11). He wrote that "that after the waters [of Noah] had receded from off the face of this land it became a choice land above all other lands, a chosen land of the Lord" (v. 2) and that "a New Jerusalem should be built up upon this land, unto the remnant of the seed of Joseph" (v. 6).

In the early days of the restored Church, the Lord commanded that the saints gather there at "a land of peace, a city of refuge":

> Wherefore I, the Lord, have said, gather ye out from the eastern lands, assemble ye yourselves together ye elders of my church; go ye forth into

the western countries, call upon the inhabitants to repent, and inasmuch as they do repent, build up churches unto me. And with one heart and with one mind, gather up your riches that ye may purchase an inheritance which shall hereafter be appointed unto you. And it shall be called the New Jerusalem, a land of peace, a city of refuge, a place of safety for the saints of the Most High God; and the glory of the Lord shall be there, and the terror of the Lord also shall be there, insomuch that the wicked will not come unto it, and it shall be called Zion. (D&C 45:64–67; emphasis added.)

What did the Lord mean by the "western countries"? Where will this city be? We are told that it will be in Jackson County, Missouri, and in the counties round about.

And in order that all things be prepared before you, observe the commandment which I have given concerning these things—which saith, or teacheth, to purchase all the lands with money, which can be purchased for money, in the region round about the land which I have appointed to be the land of Zion, for the beginning of the gathering of my saints; all the land which can be purchased in Jackson county, and the counties round about, and leave the residue in mine hand. (D&C 101:69–71; see also D&C 42:9, 35, 62–67; D&C 84:2–4; D&C 105:28–32; emphasis added.)

It is near the center of the United States of America— indeed, the Lord calls it "the center place" (see D&C57:3–5)—a place of safety established for and by His saints. It will be during a time of war.

And it shall come to pass among the wicked, that every man that will not take his sword against his neighbor must needs flee unto Zion for safety. And there shall be gathered unto it out of every nation under heaven; and it shall be the only people that shall not be at war one with another. And it shall be said among the wicked: Let us not go up to battle against Zion, for the inhabitants of Zion are terrible; wherefore we cannot stand. (D&C 45:68–70.)

The Savior also said that after Zion is established, "then shall the power of heaven come down among them; and I also will be in the midst" (see 3 Nephi 20:25). The Lord also told Enoch that He would "prepare . . . an Holy City . . . that my people may gird up their loins, and be looking forth for the time of my coming; for there shall be my tabernacle, and it shall be called Zion, a New Jerusalem" and that Enoch and "all [his] city [would] meet them there, and . . . receive them into [their] bosom" (see Moses 7:62–64).

The apostle John wrote of the New Jerusalem descending from heaven, apparently after the Millennium:

And I John saw the holy city, new Jerusalem, coming down from God out of heaven, prepared as a bride adorned for her husband. And I heard a great voice out of heaven saying, Behold, the tabernacle of God is with men, and he will dwell with them, and they shall be his people, and God himself shall be with them, and be their God. (Revelation 21:2–3.)

His description of this heavenly city is glorious. Like our father Jacob, we look "for a city which hath foundations, whose builder and maker is God" (see Hebrews 11:10).

> But now they desire a better country, that is, an heavenly: wherefore God is not ashamed to be called their God: for he hath prepared for them a city. (Hebrew 11:16.)

Finally, let me note that the prophet Ezekiel also wrote of a holy city with a temple called "The Lord Is There" (see Ezekiel 48:35). This city would be set up after the Lord's Second Coming (see Ezekiel chapters 36–48), but there are indications that this city may be established after the Millennium. It is also possible that the city he describes is the old Jerusalem, which will also be built up (see Ether 13:11).

## Chapter 31

# I Say unto All, Watch

The Savior concludes his Olivet discourse with these words: "And what I say unto you I say unto all, Watch" (Mark 13:37). We would all do well to follow His counsel, to—

Watch for signs in the heavens and signs of the times. Watch for natural disasters, scourges, and plagues. Watch for apostasy, for those rising up to steady the ark of God while decrying His work in these last days. Watch for political and economic trouble, oppression, and unrest. Watch for wars and rumors of wars. Watch the prophets and apostles of God. Watch your own thoughts, words, and actions. Watch for the Bridegroom. I'll be watching for all these things too.

This, again, is not a comprehensive guide. It is more of a personal exploration of the scriptures about the Second Coming. I invite you to make your own search. I hope the appendix of scriptural references that follows will help you in your search.

I know I have learned a lot about the Second Coming in the last year. I hope you have after reading this book as well.

Keep your lamps full and trimmed. And watch. I will too.

## Appendix

# Scriptural Passages about the Second Coming

Isaiah 2:1–22 (2 Nephi 12:1–22)

Isaiah 4:1–6 (2 Nephi 14:1–6)

Isaiah 10:1–34 (2 Nephi 20:1–34)

Isaiah 11:1–16 (2 Nephi 21:1–16)

Isaiah 12:1–6 (2 Nephi 22:1–6)

Isaiah 13:1–22 (2 Nephi 23:1–22)

Isaiah 14:1–32 (2 Nephi 24:1–32)

Isaiah 24:5–6, 20–23

Isaiah 25:1–12

Isaiah 30:25–30

Isaiah 33:1–24

Isaiah 34:1–17

Isaiah 35:4

Isaiah 40:10

Isaiah 51:19–20 (2 Nephi 8:19–20)

Isaiah 63:1–19

Isaiah 64:1–12

Isaiah 65:17–25

Isaiah 66:1–24

Daniel 7:9–10, 13–14, 18, 21–22, 27

Daniel 8:19, 23–25

Daniel 12:1–13

Joel 2:1–32

Joel 3:1–21

Nahum 1:5–6

Zephaniah 1:1–18

Zephaniah 3:1–20

Zechariah 12:1–14

Zechariah 13:1–9

Zechariah 14:1–21

Malachi 3:1–5 (3 Nephi 24:1–5)

Malachi 4:1–3 (3 Nephi 25:1–3)

Matthew 16:27

Matthew 24:1–51

Matthew 25:1–46

Matthew 26:64

Mark 8:38

Mark 13:1–37

Luke 12:39–40

Luke 17:22–37

Luke 21:1–36

Acts 1:11

Acts 3:20–21

1 Corinthians 4:5

1 Corinthians 15:24–27

Philippians 3:20

1 Thessalonians 1:10

1 Thessalonians 2:19

1 Thessalonians 3:13

1 Thessalonians 4:15–17

1 Thessalonians 5:1–7

2 Thessalonians 1:7–10

2 Thessalonians 2:1, 8

1 Timothy 6:14–16

Titus 2:13

James 5:7–8

1 Peter 1:5–7

1 Peter 4:13

2 Peter 3:10

1 John 2:28

I John 3:2

Jude 1:14–15

Revelation 6:12–17

Revelation 7:1–17

Revelation 8:1–13

Revelation 9:1–21

Revelation 10:1–11

Revelation 11:1–19

Revelation 14:1–20

Revelation 16:1–21

Revelation 20:1–15

1 Nephi 22:7–8, 16–26

2 Nephi 6:14–15

2 Nephi 8:19–20 (Isaiah 51:19–20)

2 Nephi 12:1–22 (Isaiah 2:1–22)

2 Nephi 14:1–6 (Isaiah 4:1-6)

2 Nephi 20:1–34 (Isaiah 10:1–34)

2 Nephi 21:1–16 (Isaiah 11:1–16)

2 Nephi 22:1–6 (Isaiah 12:1–6)

2 Nephi 23:1–22 (Isaiah 13:1–22)

2 Nephi 24:1–32 (Isaiah 14:1–32)

Jacob 5:70–77

3 Nephi 21:23–25

3 Nephi 24:1–5 (Malachi 3:1–5)

3 Nephi 25:1–3 (Malachi 4:1–3)

3 Nephi 26:3–4

3 Nephi 28:7–8

3 Nephi 29:2

Ether 13:1–11

D&C 1:1–17

D&C 29:9–30

D&C 33:17–18

D&C 34:5–12

D&C 39:15–24

D&C 43:30–33

D&C 45:30–71

D&C 49:5–7, 22–28

D&C 63:1–6, 32–35, 49–54

D&C 65:1–6

D&C 76:106–108

D&C 78:20–21

D&C 84:1–5, 96–102, 117–119

D&C 86:1–11

D&C 88:84–116

D&C 101:9–34

D&C 106:4–5

D&C 110:14, 16

D&C 116:1

D&C 130:14–17

D&C 133:1–74

Moses 7:60–67

Joseph Smith–Matthew 1:1–55

Articles of Faith 1:10

Made in the USA
San Bernardino, CA
13 March 2018